Preface

For centuries, Santeria has been part of life in the Americas. From the island nation of Cuba, where it first emerged, it has been disseminated throughout Latin America and has a significant presence in the United States of America. It has adherents in nations across the Atlantic – even in those nations that were once driving forces in the colonialist project of subduing the Americas.

What you'll learn in this book will challenge the popular depiction of Santeria that so many of us are accustomed to. You'll discover that Santeria is a communally-based, no hierarchical, grassroots religion and that one of its most pressing aims is to make its followers better people.

You'll learn about a religion that has withstood external distortion and defamation and even a US court case to retain the right to its religious practices. You'll meet, in this book, a Santeria you never imagined existed.

Join me for the fascinating journey into the heart of Santeria, a religion that neither colonialism nor communism could vanquish, and which today boasts millions of believers all over the world.

Clara Robinson

Santeria

Afro-Caribbean Religion and its Origins

© Copyright 2021 - All rights reserved.

In no way is it legal to reproduce, duplicate, or transmit any part of this document in either electronic means or in printed format. Recording of this publication is strictly prohibited and any storage of this document is not allowed unless with written permission from the publisher. All rights reserved.

The information provided herein is stated to be truthful and consistent, in that any liability, in terms of inattention or otherwise, by any usage or abuse of any policies, processes, or directions contained within is the solitary and utter responsibility of the recipient reader. Under no circumstances will any legal responsibility or blame be held against the publisher for any reparation, damages, or monetary loss due to the information herein, either directly or indirectly.

Respective authors own all copyrights not held by the publisher.

Legal Notice:

This ebook is copyright protected. This is only for personal use. You cannot amend, distribute, sell, use, quote or paraphrase any part or the content within this ebook without the consent of the author or copyright owner. Legal action will be pursued if this is breached.

Disclaimer Notice:

Please note the information contained within this document is for educational and entertainment purposes only. Every attempt has been made to provide accurate, up to date and reliable complete information. No warranties of any kind are expressed or implied. Readers acknowledge that the author is not engaging in the rendering of legal, financial, medical, or professional advice.

By reading this document, the reader agrees that under no circumstances are we responsible for any losses, direct or indirect, which are incurred as a result of the use of information contained within this document, including, but not limited to, —errors, omissions, or inaccuracies.

Table of Contents

Introduction

Santeria has captured the imagination of the West since it first came to be, confronting Western colonialism with the power of a folk religion derived from ancient Yoruba beliefs in West Africa, blended with Roman Catholic symbols and saints.

Called "the way of the saints," "regla lucuma," and the "rule of the orisha," Santeria created a system of belief and worship that gave enslaved people hope in the New World. Like related belief systems, Voudon, Candomble, and spiritism, Santeria is often mischaracterized as being associated with witchcraft and the dark arts.

Unsanctioned by the colonialists and springing from the enslaved, Santeria has always been viewed with suspicion, with hair-raising tales of its practices breathlessly told over centuries. For the colonialists, there was nothing more frightening than the thought of enslaved people and people whose nations were being colonized, creating their own framework of belief. Divergence was not well-tolerated by colonialism who deployed Roman Catholicism and Anglicanism (primarily) to subdue the populations whose land and resources it sought to control.

But what is Santeria really about? What do these people believe, and why did they feel it was so important to create their own belief system?

This book, Santeria: Afro-Caribbean religion and its origins, is offered in the interest of telling a story too often distorted and sensationalized. Its contents are based on historical facts and the truth about what Santeria means to its practitioners.

As we explore Santeria (as it truly is), it's helpful to keep in mind that history is written by the victors. And so, Santeria is a casualty of that effect, with the European colonialists writing the history of religion they know very little about.

Not witchcraft, not black magic, and not malevolent in any discernable way, Santeria is a recognized faith system. With no central authority, though, it's difficult to gauge the proliferation of Santeria around the world. Some estimates say there are 100s of millions of practitioners. More conservative estimates claim approximately 10 million, mostly in Latin America but with as many as 5 million in the USA.

So, let's explore this African Traditional Religion (ATR), Santeria, its beliefs, and practices, to find out the truth about one of the most misunderstood religions in the world.

Chapter 1: Out of Africa, Cuba-bound

When the Trans-Atlantic Slave Trade first arrived in Cuba from Spain in the 16th Century, there were fewer than 10,000 enslaved people in the island nation. But by just before the mid-point of the 19th Century, Cuba hosted about 400,000 enslaved people.

Coming primarily from West African, many of the enslaved were members of the Yoruba ethnic group, still found in Benin, Nigeria, and Togo (collectively call "Yorubaland").

With its own language, Yoruba is one of Africa's largest ethnic identities. There is also a Yoruba religion, which forms the foundation of Santeria.

Referred as "the source of our tradition," Yoruba religion is called Isese in the eponymous language. Landing in Cuba, the enslaved brought with them beliefs that defined their culture and society. People stripped of every vestige of personhood have little to cling to. Old songs. Old Stories. The comfort of what the enslaved Yoruba knew as they arrived in the New World, was like an umbilical cord, stretching across the ocean to distant West Africa.

An animist religion, Isese teaches that all people are governed by fate and that our common destiny is to merge with the Creator – Olodumare (Orurun) – from whom all energy emanates and to whom all energy returns. Isese also teaches that humans are intended to perfect their souls in this life through acts of charity and adherence to the tenets and ceremonial of Isese. In this perfection of the soul, they reach the spiritual balance that defines a lifetime of attending the needs of the human spirit and the project of its perfection.

In Isese, the spiritual self is not unlike a reflection of God. The belief that we return to the source of all (especially, all energy) upon death extends the Isese belief that human beings are less "children" of God and more "cousins." This conceptualization of the God-human relationship implies the accountability of adulthood. Today, the Yoruba Faith is not only practiced in its traditional setting in West Africa. It's also practiced in Haiti, Trinidad and Tobago, and Brazil.

Now that we know a little about the Yoruba religion – one of Santeria's parent Faiths – let's talk about what happened in Cuba. Why was this new Faith created?

A New Faith for a New World

When the colonialists shared their Old European religion with the enslaved, it was greeted with a measure of acceptance. However, this did not mean that the enslaved were entirely given to renouncing the beliefs of their West African Faith.

To the contrary, the slaves listened with interest to the tales told them of the God born of a woman into flesh, killed by crucifixion, and raised from that death to be the Savior of the human soul. And they drew from the beliefs they were being taught what pleased them, weaving it into the beliefs of Isese.

In that weaving are the origins of Santeria.

But much of how Santeria was originally established had to do with the colonialists and the Roman Catholic Church. The Church, dedicated as it was to the inculturation of native populations in "conquered" regions, made space for native beliefs and, in the case of the enslaved, imported beliefs.

Because of this unusually tolerant tendency of the Church in Cuba, the Cabildos were formed. Cabildos were used as ethnic associations but also as centers of African beliefs and their practice. Leadership was in the hands of the "babalawo," who was the religious leader tending the flock in each Cabildo. However, this leadership was obscured from the Church, allowing the Cabildos to operate without interference.

Arising from these ethnic organizations was a point of contact between the Catholic Church and the Yoruba religion. The Cabildos used the liturgical calendar of the Church to venerate the saints of Africa, adhering to the Church's worship rhythms while dedicating them to other purposes.

In this crucible of human enslavement and colonialism, Santeria emerged, Yoruba practitioners having been provided with a tent of meeting in the wilderness by the colonial Church itself. Colonial Cuba's cultural cauldron bubbled until it boiled over in a new expression of faith in the ostensibly syncretic religion, Santeria.

Turning (not entirely) from the beliefs of the colonialists, enslaved people, their identities and names and languages stripped from them took instead the seeds of a Faith that would form the basis of a new religion. Santeria incorporated some of the beliefs and practices of Holy Mother Church but was conspicuously oriented toward Mother Africa. And the more you know about

Santeria, the less evident the Catholic influence becomes because the truth is that it was used primarily as cover for the West African religion, which was being transformed to become an entirely new one.

Catholic saints became representations of the orishas (emanations or manifestations of Olomudare) of Yoruba. This practice pursued to lend the appearance of compliance with colonialist wishes led to the superficial syncretism between the two belief systems, which emerged as Santeria.

Castro's Ban and Cuban Santeria Today

Following the Cuban Revolution, religion of all kinds was banned, including Santeria. This ban remained in place from 1959 until 1992.

While 27% of Cubans today are Roman Catholic, 13% are followers of Santeria. Most Cubans, though, don't follow any religion at all. That said, both religions exert tremendous cultural influence in Cuba, with most Cubans holding beliefs from both Faiths.

But about 80% of Cubans hold to some practices of Santeria, while only 1% of Cubans attend Catholic Mass with any regularity. It's clear then where Cuba's heart is. This becomes even clearer when you consider that many of the saints depicted in Cuban churches have counterparts in the orishas of Santeria and that most of the people at Mass are most likely to be santeros (practitioners).

This should come as no surprise. Fully 20% of the Cuban population is descended from the enslaved people who carried the Yoruba Faith to the New World in their hearts. For modern Cubans, especially those of African descent, Santeria stands as a symbol of defiance in the face of oppression and of the continuation of generations of belief in a modified package. It also stands as a link to Mother Africa and between the lost generations of peoples translated to Cuba's shores over hundreds of years.

Some Basics

Everyone's heard a story or two about Santeria (or Voudon or Candomble). But the stories that circulate about Faiths that diverge from the major monotheist Faiths, especially when they emerge as new, ostensibly syncretic religions, are usually based on misinformation.

This misinformation is often perpetrated for the sake of defaming Santeria and other associated religions. And why? Not just because of competing for followers but because Santeria has its roots in Africa.

But Santeria is not Pagan, witchcraft, or black magic. Santeria is a religion with its roots in African religion, with some imagery and ideas from Catholicism woven into it. Let's look at some of the core beliefs of Santeria.

- **One Creator God**

Santeria is monotheistic, believing in only one God – Olodumare (the God of Yoruba). The orisha is a reflection of God and God's attributes and more akin to saints than to a pantheon of lesser gods (as some erroneously claim).

- **Ancestral Veneration**

Ancestral veneration is a central practice in Santeria. Before every ritual or ceremony, drink offerings are poured out for the ancestors. Ancestral veneration is a common feature of most African (and global indigenous) Faith traditions.

- **Communally Focused**

The community is central to the practice of Santeria. Ceremonies and rituals are led by trained priests, usually descended from a line of Santeria priests in the family. One becomes a priest only after years of dedicated study. The order of priests includes the Babalawo, Santero, and olorisha.

- **Arduous Initiation**

  Becoming a santero is no joke. A year and a week of your time are required, and while the initiation is in progress, you're under stringent rules of conduct, including what you may consume, what you may wear, and how you are to conduct yourself.

Induction into Santeria is no trifling affair. There is no effort on the part of practitioners to convert people to the religion. It's an individual matter which must be undertaken with great gravity of purpose. Because once you're in, you have responsibilities.

The Santeria initiation is a soulful experience of entering a new world of spirituality as a new creature. For that reason, initiates are subject to rules like not being permitted out after dark, having to wear shoes at all times, having to wear white, and a period of fasting. In addition, initiates must be focused on spiritual matters continually and passionately during the year plus a week of initiation.

Upon completion of their year of spiritual trial and initiation, novice santeros are considered "re-born."

- **The Heart of Santeria**

   There are two concepts at the very heart of the practice of Santeria that is crucial to understanding its intent and purpose as a religion.

   The first of these is Ashe (also Axe, Ache, or Ase). Ashe is a "life force." Ashe is a gift from Olodumare which animates us and fills our souls with creative energy and the ability to live through life's most difficult moments. For this reason, all santeros are considered "cousins" of Olodumare, as the Creator is the source of Ashe.

   The second concept is Iwa Pele, which means to live in kindness and humility. This is very similar to the Christian concept of a "state of grace." Living this way, santeros learn to work on their flaws and to become the best people they can possibly be, sending positive, humble, kind energy into the world around them.

- ## The Truth about Animal Sacrifice

Animals are sacrificed in Santeria but not with the frequency, brutality, or other sensationalistic flourishes popular culture claims.

The practice of animal sacrifice in Santeria is not wanton or disrespectful to the animal. In fact, animals sacrificed in the religion as part of a ritual are blessed, prayed over, and then sacrificed in the same way a Halal (Muslim) or Kosher (Jewish) butcher would slaughter an animal. The blessing, in Santeria, is in the blood, as this is food set aside for the orishas themselves. The congregation consumes the meat.

After an animal sacrifice, it's usually the practice that the meat of the animal will be eaten by those in attendance at the ceremony or ritual, except in the case of a death or illness.

- ## Home Is the Temple

If you're a student of world religions, you'll know that the Early Christians worshipped in their homes. Santeros do the same.

There are no churches or temples for practitioners. While santeros attend Catholic masses, these are not their houses of worship but an adjunct to the practice of creating ceremonial and ritual events in the home or in another communal space (usually in the open and public).

Each practitioner has an orisha to whom they turn for guidance. This is part of the individual santero's worship. Included are ancestral veneration, as well as divination (passed down from generation to generation but now enshrined in printed form, as books). Like many indigenous systems of Faith, it's the individual and that individual's immediate context that is the focus of worship, much of which is devoted to seeking guidance from the orishas and ancestors.

In addition to home worship, there are also public ceremonies encompassing the community of believers in the area as well as others. Those not initiated are invited to stand behind the santeros and to keep far away from the drums, which are inhabited by the orisha, Anya.

- **A Song for Every Ceremony**

  All public ceremonies in Santeria are accompanied by drumming and singing, and each ceremony has a specific song associated with it. The more people are singing, the better the Ashe, and so, everyone is encouraged to sing to elevate the Ashe of the ceremony in play.

  As the drums are consecrated, and Anya causes them to speak, the priests present to host the orisha, the sound of Anya calling from the drums drawing them. As the subject of the gathering (who has offered themselves to be possessed) are possessed by the orisha, the priests act as conduits for the knowledge and advice the orisha have brought with them for the congregation, interpreting it.

These are the most central facts about Santeria and its beliefs and practices. From here, we can move on to a detailed exploration of key facets of this religion. As you can see, Santeria is a survivor of sorts, embodying the dreams of a people removed from their lives and contexts to build a new reality on behalf of those who took them for labor. From that experience of oppression and abuse, Santeria rose, representing the strength and power of Africa in the New World. And to this day, that strength and power continue in this fascinating faith expression.

Next, let's look at Santeria in more depth and discover for ourselves the truth about Santeria.

Chapter 2: Meet the Orishas

The orishas are not gods. The orishas are facets of the Divine. They all represent a certain sphere of life and the qualities of God associated with that sphere. The orishas also act as "patron saints" for santeros. Following initiation, every santero has their orisha revealed to them. This will be their patron throughout their lives.

One of the most important things I need to tell you about orishas is that Catholic saints served as camouflage for them. As I said in the last chapter, the Cabildos were used as gathering places and also as places where the Yoruba faith could be practiced in secret. Slave-owners weren't in accord with the Church about the possibility of the enslaved practicing a native Faith – it was dangerous. Such worship would only serve to remind the enslaved that they were human beings with their own ideas. And so, Santeria and other Faiths incorporating elements of the foundational Faith systems from which they were built were suppressed if they weren't hidden.

That's why the saints acted as "beards" or perhaps, "saintly shields" for the saints of Africa. The saints of the Catholic Church provided something along the lines of a plastic mustache, obscuring the identity of the subject of veneration.

And this was and is perfectly in keeping with Yoruba's conceptualization of the orisha. The orisha "hide," appearing to us under alternative guises. Masquerading as the saints of the Catholic Church was nothing new. In fact, the orishas are known for this quality of obscuring themselves to achieve a specific end.

This tendency to disguise themselves also worked as a means of helping practitioners understand what the orishas were doing and why. There was a method to the madness, and in the New World, there was a noble purpose – to hide the truth about the Faith being practiced so that the enslaved might worship in peace.

The orishas number in the hundreds in their original (Yoruba) context. In the New World, their ranks have been pared down somewhat. Following are orishas you should know about.

Aganyu

This orisha is fiery and ferocious, responsible for events like earthquakes and volcanic eruptions. Called up for assistance with fevers, Aganyu's color is read.

Santeria and Yoruba lore describe Aganyu as a ferryman, taking his ferry across a river. For this reason, he's associated with travel and the protection of travelers. S. Christopher is thus considered his parallel Catholic saint. Some practitioners also associate Aganyu with S. Joseph (father of Jesus) and the Archangel Michael.

While Michael has his sword, Aganyu has a double-edged ax. The horns of a bull may also represent Aganyu.

Babalu-Aye

This humble, compassionate orisha is the patron of the sick, the poor, and those living with physical and mental challenges.

But Babalu-Aye plays both sides of the street, being just as willing to inflict illness as to cure it. The orisha is often represented as being covered in open sores, so many associate him with the curing (or infliction) of skin infections.

The Biblical character, Lazarus, is associated with Babalu-Aye. In the Medieval Era, the name of Lazarus was often invoked by people suffering from leprosy.

Babalu-Aye's colors are purple and light blue, and his symbols are cowrie shells, dogs, reeds, and crutches.

Chango

Chango is not to be messed with. He is the orisha of lightning, thunder, and fire. He is ever on guard to exact revenge against the enemies of those who call on him. But Chango doesn't like to be trifled with. Don't tick him off, or you may be incinerated by one either lightning or fire.

This orisha can go either way – to the good or to the bad. Rageful and arrogant, he is the source of both justice and vengeance. Known as sexually robust, Chango rules over the sexuality of men, virility, and male fertility.

Oggun, Chango's brother, rules over metal and especially iron. Nothing to do with iron may be brought into Chango's presence.

Chango's Catholic parallels are S. Barbara (primarily), S. Mark, S. Jerome, S. Bartholomew, S. Elijah, and S. Expeditus. His symbols are the thunderbolt, the castle, the double-edged ax (like Aganyu), and the cup. Colors associated with Chango are red and white.

Eleggua

After Obatala, Eleggua (also called "Eshu") is the most powerful of all orishas. Elggua opens doors, bringing supplicants to new horizons. He is a warrior, a trickster, and a messenger, offering protection to travelers.

Eleggua is also the ruler of the crossroads (where the world of the spirits meets the world of the living). He is a potent seer and keeper of mysteries and secrets. This orisha is mischievous (trickster role) and clever but also childlike. Conditions of the blood and accidents are attributable to Eleggua.

All Santeria ceremonies and rituals begin with offerings to Eleggua, as he is the conduit governing affairs between humans and the orishas. As the opener of doorways, he also rules over communication, bearing the petitions of human practitioners to the orishas.

Eleggua is sometimes known to lead people down the garden path, goading them to try alternative means of achieving the ends of their supplications. Sometimes, these are very bad ideas. But he's a trickster, so being aware of that status is helpful.

Sometimes, Eleggua disguises himself as a child. For this reason, he's often associated with S. Anthony (depicted carrying the child Jesus) and Benito, the Infant of Prague, and S. Martin Porres.

Eleggua's colors are red and black, and his symbols are a whistle or a red and black crook (hooked staff used by shepherds).

Obatala

In the Yoruba Faith, Obatala was asked by Olodumare to create the earth and is one of the oldest of all the orishas. The position of this orisha is adjacent to the Creator.

Obatala is considered an orisha of purity, and so all offerings to this orisha should be of white food or white birds (when animals are to be sacrificed as part of the ritual). No spices are to be used in any of the foods offered, and the altar and santeros should be dressed in white.

Depictions of Obatala show the orisha in white clothes, wearing a white crown and carrying a staff, painted white. This orisha is not considered male or female but generally favors female practitioners.

Obatala's Catholic counterpart is Our Lady of Mercy. This orisha is also closely associated with Jesus (see Obatala's co-creative role in the Yoruba/Santeria Faiths above). In Santeria, this orisha fulfills the role of "Son of God" in tandem with that of the Mother of the Son of God.

A famous tale about Fidel Castro highlights the importance of Santeria in Cuba. During a speech in 1959, two white doves flew over the podium, with one landing on Castro's shoulder. The dove is a symbol of Obatala, and so this was considered an auspicious symbol of Olodumare's favor.

Yemaya

The patron of women and motherhood, Yemaya is the orisha of water and bodies of water. The spiritual mother of everyone, Yemaya is nurturing and dignified.

Yemaya is also representing mystery, as embodied by the element of water, its depth, its life-giving properties, and its relentless but gentle effect on the natural world. Yemaya rules over intestinal disorders and tuberculosis.

The sister of Oshun, Yemaya's Catholic parallel, is Our Lady of Reglas, who protects sailors. Like the Virgin Mary in Catholicism, Yemaya's colors are blue and white.

Oshun

Yemaya's sister, Oshun, rules over the lower abdomen and genitalia. Seductive and beautiful, Oshun is associated with the beauty of women, marriage, love, and fertility. Oshun, like her sister, is also associated with water but only fresh water sources, like rivers.

Oshun is known in Santeria lore for saving the world from drought after the orishas conspired to try and get rid of Olodumare and the Creator dried the earth. Oshun became a peacock and begged for Olodumare's forgiveness, which the Creator God gave her - water was restored to the earth due to Oshun's intervention.

Her parallel in Catholicism is Our Lady of Charity, who is also the patron saint of Cuba. Oshun is represented by a mirror, peacock feather, boat, or fan. Her colors are violet, yellow, coral, amber, red, and green.

Orunla

Orisha of human destiny and divination, Orunla does not respond to supplications to manifest in ritual possession – in the New World. In Africa, it's known to happen.

Orunla was there as humans were created and received their souls. This allows him to foresee the destiny of each human. Because santeros believe that destiny is something we work towards, perfecting ourselves to promote harmony, this is a crucial point in the beliefs of the religion. Orunla rules over divination.

This orisha's Catholic counterpart is S. Francis of Assisi, as well as S. Philip and S. Joseph, with Francis being the most common correlation. This is believed to be because S. Francis is commonly depicted holding rosary beads, a parallel to Orunla's divination chain.

Orunla's colors are green and yellow. He is represented by the Table of Ifa, Santeria's most complicated divination methodology.

Osain

Herbalism, healing, and nature are Osain's reign. The patron of hunter and home, Osain is a contrast to most icons associated with nature, being rational and collected instead of wild.

Osain is depicted as having only one eye in the middle of his face. Because he has lost an eye, an ear, an arm, and a leg, his symbol is the gnarled branch of a tree, which he uses as a crutch. Osain's colors are white, yellow, green, and red. Associated with Pope S. Sylvester I, he's also paired with S. John, S. Anthony Abad, and S. Joseph, among others.

Oya

This is the orisha of the dead and is called upon for guidance in all matters concerning cemeteries, ancestors, and wind. Oya is a strong, ferocious orisha, reigning over electrocution and windstorms.

Oya also oversees change and transitions. A warrior, Oya is often depicted wearing clothing gendered male so she can ride into war with Chango. It's said that Oya is the true ruler of fire but that she allows Chango's stewardship of it.

In Catholicism, Oya's parallel is Our Lady of Candlemas, as well as S. Teresa and Our Lady of Mt. Carmel. Her symbols are a nine-pointed copper crown, a lance, fire, and black horsetail, and her color is maroon.

These are the principle orishas. What's important to note is that, while Yoruba includes at least 400 orishas, in Cuba, only 20 are recognized.

The orishas are not only sought out by santeros for guidance; they're also blamed for personal misfortune. In the instance of misfortune, practitioners of Santeria will seek to appease the orisha in question.

With the assistance of the Babalawo, the santero will seek contact with their orisha (as assigned at initiation). Using divination, these Santeria priests interpret the will of the orishas. The ceremony of divination may include drumming, the use of rum and cigars, and animal sacrifice, in some instances.

In Santeria, orishas are not considered divine but rather reflections or manifestations of the Creator God, Olodumare. For that reason, it's believed that if people don't call on the orishas that they cease to exist. And so, the existence of the orishas is entirely dependent on human devotion and interaction, mediated by the Babalawos and others of the Santeria priestly class.

The power of ritual is at the center of Santeria. Not having any grand cathedrals or points of a formal meeting, Santeria is a folk religion with a grassroots following, circumscribed by culture but not exclusive in terms of who may practice (with the usual year and a week-long ritual considered).

Santeria also has no holy books. There is no Bible. There is no Quran. The entirety of this religion was passed down orally, just as the books of the Bible originally were until they were eventually codified and then canonized.

For this reason, ritual and ceremony are key factors in Santeria worship. While this is true to a degree of all religions, in Santeria, it's the ritual that bears the hopes and prayers of the people. Just as with an Order of Mass, with its Bible readings, hymns, credal recitations, and ritual heartbeat, Santeria practice comes to life in the community. And while there are no official houses of worship for the ritual life of Santeria to be realized, the communal nature of the religion makes public spaces a natural fit. There is no need to close a door because there are no doors. There is no need to hide any longer. There is only the need of the people gathered in community and in faith and the work of the priests, bearing forward offerings and sacrifice and interpreting the will of the orishas and the Creator from whom they emanate.

In our next chapter, we'll be discussing two important features of Santeria, which are trance possession and divination. We've touched on both briefly here and there so far, but now we'll take a deep dive into these Santeria practices, finding out what they mean and how they're deployed.

Chapter 3: Trance Possession and Divination in Santeria

In this chapter, we'll explore two aspects of Santeria that have attracted a lot of attention from the outside world – trance possession and divination. Trance possession is the offering of a member of the Santeria community to be possessed by an orisha. Divination is the practice of consulting with the orishas and ergun (ancestors) through the agency of an ordained priest in the Faith.

Both practices are viewed with suspicion outside the fold – either that or prurient interest. But these practices form a vital part of worship in Santeria and are to be treated with the utmost respect. Curiosity is no excuse for interpolating yourself into the ritual practice of a Faith unless you're willing to model such respect, so please keep this in mind as you read.

While science has attempted to explain trance possession as a kind of vulnerability in some human brains, millions of people all over the world swear to have experienced trance possession. And in Santeria, it's a huge part of the religion's ritual makeup.

Trance possession in Santeria is used for the purpose of gaining the ears of the orishas through the priestly work of the Babalawo. The priest interprets what the orisha has revealed and, in turn, reveals it to the santeros present.

But it's the santeros themselves in whom trances are induced. In fact, this is one of the distinguishing features of those trained to be Babalawos – that they are impervious to trances.

The trance, induced by song and ceremony, is one of the most vital experiences for practitioners of Santeria. In falling into a trance, the santero has surrendered, offering a human vessel for the messages of the orishas. This is a holy status, signifying the surrender of the self to the purposes and will of God through the Divine manifestations of the orishas.

But it's not only a message that's experienced in trance possession – it's the actual possession of a human body by the orisha being called upon for guidance.

Santeros will be the first to admit that there are "fakes" attracted to the religion for the purpose of aggrandizing themselves. But part of being a santero is the development of spiritual discernment. This superpower of the spiritually inclined enables practitioners of all Faiths to see through the machinations of interlopers and phonies who have no respect for the religion or the people practicing it. And so, with the bona fide come the wannabes – a common occupational hazard in any religion.

In the instance of trance possession, the community takes center stage as part of the ritual. Trance possession being witnessed by the community of believers is considered a tremendous moment in the life of the community. This brings everyone participating into the enfleshed presence of an orisha in the act of "riding" a "caballo" (horse – the person under trance possession). And this is a key point when discussing trance possession in Santeria – that it benefits the whole community in attendance.

In Community

Trance possession is a community affair. All members of the community attend knowing what to expect and are accustomed to the process. They're able to recognize when a trance possession is taking hold.

When the signs of possession are noted, the community gathers around the santero undergoing trance, chanting, dancing, and invoking the name of the orisha being invited to possess the individual involved.

Trance possession often appears frightening to outsiders. The possessed person may exhibit signs of distress, like running aimlessly around the area or falling to the floor, shaking.

At the heart of trance, possession is the "toque." The toque is a drum rhythm played for a specific orisha. The person who is the subject of the ritual will be possessed, but others may be as well, especially if the toque is played for their orisha (the one assigned at initiation). In any ceremony in which the drums are played, many people in the community may be possessed, and a variety of orishas may present themselves in this way, regardless of the toque. These manifestations follow the assigned orishas of each person possessed.

Once trance possession has been established in the subject of the ritual, the possessed person is removed from the ceremony, and the priestly Santeros take over. They will all be ceremonially dressed according to the orisha who's been invited to "ride the caballo" (be possessed).

The orishas possess both men and women, regardless of the sex traditionally associated with the orisha in question. This results in gendered traits being exhibited. Women possessed by a traditionally male orisha will, for example, exhibit characteristics associated with gendered masculinity in their body language and vocal expression. Men will take on traits traditionally associated with gendered femininity when possessed by an orisha sexed as female. They will become more fluid in their movements and exhibit classically feminine body language and vocal expression.

Partying with the Orishas

Once trance possession has taken hold, the orishas raise the roof. They're part of the community and join the party in their human bodies, partaking of all the fun. They dance, sing, chat, and enjoy the food and drink. They're also known to dispense counsel and to greet people by name.

This is an experience prized in Santeria communities everywhere, as it's an opportunity to know the orishas. Temporarily enfleshed, they come into the community as one of the faithful yet exhibiting all the characteristics associated with the orisha who has taken possession of the human caballo.

It's a party, alright, but it's a party with an honored guest (or guests) – the enfleshed orisha.

It is, therefore, a sacred moment for santeros, having been honored by the presence of an emanation of the Creator.

A Human Vessel

Trance possession offers santeros a direct experience of the orishas, the emanations of Olodumare, the Creator. And the human body is the medium that makes such an experience possible.

The human body, in Santeria, is more than the sum of its parts. It has a function beyond biology. In trance possession, the soul of the caballo temporarily leaves to create space for trance possession by the Orisha being called out to.

This is both a sacrifice and a profound honor for the person being possessed. By relinquishing control of their person to the orisha, the santero is making a sacrifice for the sake of the community's wellbeing by making space for an emanation of the Divine. In so doing, the possessed person is coddled by the orisha, who brings healing and comfort while the trance possession is in progress.

For outsiders, trance possession may appear unduly violent, with the caballo in a state of what appears to be distress. But this distress is the relinquishment of personal autonomy and the replacement of that autonomy by an external spiritual reality – the orisha. The self-sacrificial nature of trance possession is most evident in this relinquishment of personal autonomy.

When the ritual concludes, the drums are stilled, and the caballo returns to normal consciousness, exhausted. As this stage of the process occurs, the community again gathers around the person who's been "ridden," comforting them and ensuring that no harm comes to them. The caballo is then taken away from the ritual area to a place where they can rest and recover from the experience of being possessed.

As I explained earlier, not all santeros will undergo trans possession. Either they're unwilling, or they're not meant to partake of the ceremony. This is the fundamental requirement for a Babalawo – that they not be vulnerable to possession.

People in attendance who are uninitiated are sometimes known to fall into trance possession. This is discouraged, as the power of Ache (the life force) can't be absorbed by those uninitiated into Santeria. When this happens, the person falling into a trance is removed from the ritual space to a place where the drums can't be heard and brought back to normal consciousness.

Divination

Divination in Santeria is the legacy of a Yoruba practice. The concept behind divination is to forge a link between heaven and earth, bringing guidance to the community in times of transition and profound change in the lives of individual members. The orishas and ergun (ancestors) are both sought out using divination. Palm nuts are sometimes used for this purpose or a halved coconut. Whatever objects are being used, the manner in which the pieces fall is the subject of the practice of divination.

Santeria priests (Olorishas) are charged with divination, but only the most senior male priests (the Babalawo) may use the intact system of divination utilized in Yoruba, which is called "Ifa." With Ifa, the ekwele (which is a chain consisting of 8 links), is used and the manner in which it falls guides the Babalowa's interpretation. We'll talk more about Ifa shortly.

Only those ordained to the priesthood may perform divination, as it's a highly specialized facet of Santeria, and all objects used to accomplish it are consecrated to the ritual.

It's also important to remember when talking about divination in Santeria that Ache is a key component in interpretation and the forging of the link between earth and heaven. Ache is the life force, and to be able to perform what's required in divination, the Ache of the priest must be called. Divination is a sacred vocation, not fortune-telling, a trick with mirrors or crystal ball gazing.

There are several ways to go about divination, so let's find out what they are.

Dilogun

Dilogun is cowrie shells that have been consecrated and are used by the Olorishas for divination during what's called a consulta or a registro (consultation or "checkup"). Anyone can seek out an Olorisha. This is usually pursued in times of uncertainty or anxiety. The Olorisha's job is to establish whether the person requesting the divination is blessed (ire) or osorbo (obstructed). If the result of the divination is the presence of osorbo, the Olorisha will advise as to the source of the problem and the cause and then offer suggestions for how to get rid of the obstruction. Even in the case of ire, the client will be given advice as to how to keep the blessings flowing.

As a consultation/checkup unfolds, the Olorisha may discern other needs the client has concerning work, family, friends, marriage, safety, and other personal matters. But the same client may be warned by the Olorisha about any bad behavior on their part that the divination has revealed. When the client is faithful (following the priest's advice), the orishas will intervene to guide them toward the spiritual development they require. But if the client is faithless (doesn't follow the priest's advice), matters will get worse.

Usually, 16 cowrie shells that belong to the orisha, Eleggua, will be used. It's Eleggua's role to facilitate communication with the other orishas and ancestors. So, any orisha might offer a "hot take" when the Dilogun is thrown.

Regla De Ifa

Regla de Ifa is a system running parallel to Santeria, originating in West Africa. In the Regla de Ifa, only men who are heterosexual may be initiated, after which initiation, they're known as Babalawos (priests of Orunla, who rule over divination and the Babalawo priestly class but never presents during trance possessions).

In Ifa divination, as I've mentioned earlier in this chapter, a chain called a ekuele (or epuele), consisting of 8 pieces, is thrown. As with Dilogun, the patterns revealed when the ekuele is thrown decide whether the client is either blessed or obstructed.

Only Babalawos are permitted to work directly with Orunla, who is the repository of the world's secrets and the master diviner.

Obi

Obi is coconut divination and is often referred to as "dar coco" (to consult with the coconut). In Yoruba culture, the coconut is considered sacred.

In a traditional consulta, the Olorisha cuts open a coconut with either a mallet or a machete. The coconut must not be placed or thrown on the floor to open it but must be held in the priest's hands.

Once open, the Olorisha selects 4 pieces of the broken coconut of about the same size. These will be trimmed to make the pieces easier to manage. As the ritual proceeds with prayers, the Olorisha throws the pieces of obi to render yes or no answers to simple questions. This type of divination is usually used to address the desires of the orishas, determining what they require in terms of offerings, where to place the offerings, and whether the orishas approve of the offerings after they've been made.

No Laughing Matter

The consulta/registro is no laughing matter. It's not there to amuse curiosity seekers. While Santeria welcomes outsiders seeking guidance, those who request a "checkup" must undertake divination seriously and with the intention of following the advice, they're being given by the priest.

Olorishas and Babalawos are highly trained and invested with a level of Ache that commands your respect. Go only with that respect in your mind and heart, and be prepared to take the advice you're given as the result of the divination.

Also, be prepared to hear about factors in your life you need to reform. Go ready to grow, to change, and to move toward the kind of life that is a blessing in itself. Santeria's central goal is to perfect and hone the spirit to its highest form, and if you're interested in that, a consulta/registro may be for you. If not, please don't play. Santeria is a religion just like any other, and if you wouldn't walk into your parents' house of worship with an attitude, don't do that with Santeria's rituals and ceremonies.

In our next and final chapter, we'll explore animal sacrifice in Santeria, why it's practiced, and the purpose it serves.

Chapter 4: Animal Sacrifice in Santeria

This next chapter may be a little difficult for some to read. Most of us love animals. We love our dogs, our cats, our gerbils, our budgies, and our pet goats. But most of us also eat animals or otherwise use animal byproducts in our daily lives. Those of us who don't may find the practice of animal sacrifice problematic.

But animal sacrifice, while central to the practice of Santeria, is not what it may seem to be on the surface. Like trance possession and divination, we might find the practice difficult to wrap our heads around.

But if you read the Bible, you'll know that animal sacrifice was practiced in the ancient Temple in Jerusalem. While animal sacrifice is no longer part of Judaism, the fact that it ever existed will give you a bit of perspective in the confrontation of what you're about to read.

Animal sacrifices are reserved for special occasions in Santeria, including weddings, funerals, and births. The practice is also sometimes used to request healing from the orishas. But the principal purpose of these sacrifices is not the spectacle or the desire to kill an animal. The principal purpose is to provide food (blood) to the orishas and to bless the community of believers. The initiation of new believers and the consecration of priests are also occasions for animal sacrifice.

Ritual slaughter in Santeria is the same as it is in religions like Judaism and Islam, with the carotid artery being cut in a single swipe of the knife. After the animal is killed, it is cooked and eaten. The only time this is not the case is in the instance of illness (when the animal has been slaughtered to promote healing) and death. As the animal is eaten, the community of the faithful is sharing a meal with the orishas. The orishas do not eat the flesh of the animals but the blood, which is why the method of ritual slaughter is used – to extract as much blood as possible for the orishas. The community eats the flesh.

Animals eaten at Santeria rituals are chickens, ducks, guinea pigs, sheep, turtles, goats, doves, and pigeons.

The Sacred Life Force

The letting of blood is tied to the human knowledge (even before science) that the blood in our bodies is what gives us life. Accidents, skirmishes between rival humans, and wars cemented this belief, as the letting of blood came to be synonymous with the concept of sacrifice – the sacrifice of a human or animal life for the good of the community.

In ritual, sacrifice is an ancient human impulse to give something to the unseen world of the spirits to protect itself, to bring good fortune, or to put an end to misfortune. In Santeria, the bloodletting is reserved for the sole use of the orishas, while the community shares in the meal by consuming the flesh of the sacrificed animal. Thus, the human community shares in the bounty occasioned by the sacrifice of the animals with the orishas themselves. In sharing a meal brought about by the sacrifice of an animal or animals, the human world is brought into communion with the spirit world.

The word "sacrifice" means what it implies – the willing release of a resource to a sacred purpose. For instance, we sacrifice our time and money for causes we believe in. We sacrifice ourselves, bodily, to war – sometimes dying as part of the sacrifice. Sacrifice is holy in any way it's achieved. And in Santeria, the sacrifice offered is that of a vital resource that the spirit and human worlds may share together. While the sacrifice has provided blood to the orishas, it has provided material sustenance to the human community of believers.

In the sacrifice of any kind, humanity admits its frailty and dependence on the will of the Divine. It is a type of obeisance and denial of the self. Even when the sacrifice is an animal, the dedication of that animal to a ritual purpose removes it from the conglomeration of resources held by a human being for sustenance. By dedicating the animal to the use of the community (toward its betterment and the ongoing relationship with the spiritual sustenance provided by the orishas), Santeria practitioners model humility, a desire for connection with the spirit world and respect for the animal, as it is consumed in community, thus playing a leading role in maintaining the favor of the orishas and the continuing spiritual development of the worshipping community.

Maintaining a Healthy Relationship

Of pivotal importance in any discussion about animal sacrifice in Santeria is the very real fact that without animal sacrifice, religion would not be possible. There is a symbiosis between the orishas and the faithful of the religion, which would be ruptured were the practice to cease.

Closely linked to health in Santeria (which is a complex of factors like money, physical and spiritual health, and community – holistic, in other words), animal sacrifice is a component of the Santeria practitioner's agreement with the orishas. This can be loosely described as a mutually arrived at agreement, defining the duties of both parties so as not to default.

Health, in Santeria, has a strong component of spiritual and communal health, and so, animal sacrifice serves to maintain robust health, best defined by Ache – the life force, fed by all the usual material factors (exercise, good food, clean water, pleasant outlook, healthy relationships) is supported by ritual played out in the heart of the worshipping community. Maintaining the relationship and agreement between the orishas and their human supplicants is at least partially achieved through the practice of animal sacrifice.

Yoruba, in which Santeria has its roots, calls sacrifice "ebo." This word is applied to both the ritual and the animal being sacrificed. In addition, understanding that there's only one word for "sacrifice," "offering," and "purification" in the Yoruba language is instructive. This one word describes the purpose of animal sacrifice eloquently when we understand the relationship of santeros to the orishas as an agreement rooted in reciprocity – quid pro quo. The sense is that relationships bear mutual benefit, regardless of their context (religious or merely social), as well as mutual responsibility.

Also, "ebo" builds up the Ache of both the community and the orishas. In sacrificing animals to the orishas, the worshipping community receives a benefit in blessings, protection, and spiritual development.

In this state of replenished and fortified Ache, the orishas are revitalized and able to hold up their end of the ritual bargain. Having been fed and fortified, they're better equipped to regale intensified Ache on the community doing the sacrificing.

Ire and Osorbo

Ire is a state of balance, good fortune, and good, holistic health. Osorbo is the opposite, provoked by malicious spirits targeting our balance, good fortune, and good holistic health.

When all is well, it is "ire." When "osorbo" strikes, this is generally interpreted to mean that the community – or someone in the community – isn't doing what it/they are supposed to be doing. The agreement is not being upheld, and thus, there is dissonance, resulting in ill health, loss, and discord.

The interplay between these two states is considered, in Santeria, to be part of life. We take the good with the bad, and the bad isn't necessarily "all bad." This is an interesting component of the religious philosophy of Santeria, especially with respect to the idea of sacrifice. But in terms of comparative religion, it's even more interesting.

In Judaism, for example, the "yetzer ha-rah" and the "yetzer ha-tov" (evil and good impulses, respectively) are very similar to osorbo and ire. In Judaism, the idea that evil can be eliminated is unacceptable, as evil provides balance, not only materially but spiritually.

If everything around us was good, how would we understand the beauty of goodness? And if everything around us was good, how would we recognize evil? How would we defend ourselves against it? This is the burning question in the Creation narrative of Genesis in Torah: was the fall of Adam and Eve a fall up or a fall down?

In eating from the Tree of the Knowledge of Good and Evil, the Primordial Humans lost their innocence in discovering the concept of consequences being tied to disobedience. But they gained sentience and discernment. In Santeria, ire and osorbo are also understood to represent a fine balance.

Ire and osorbo are two parts of a whole. In knowing that the bad is part of human nature, we're given the gift of bettering ourselves. By claiming the darkness as well as the light, we become capable of developing ourselves spiritually and morally. Think of naïve people who've never been outside their immediate area. When confronted by the world, they're lost. They've never experienced anything but what they know, and if all you know is unending goodness, surely evil will come as a terribly nasty surprise.

And this brings us back to the subject of this final chapter – ebo (sacrifice). And that sacrifice isn't always a living thing. Sometimes what we sacrifice is simple; something that pleases the orisha we wish to attract the favor and counsel of. Any sacrifice made with an open heart attracts the compassion of the orishas.

But in some instances, the letting of blood is required by Santeria. The spilling of the life force re-balances the agreement made between humanity and the orishas. This rebalancing, in turn, addresses the presence of evil in the life of the community and the obligation of the orishas to hear the supplications of that community. In restoring balance through the practice of ebo, the balance between good and evil is restored. This acts to encourage the community toward the spiritual development that provides wellbeing and prosperity to the community and succor and sustenance to the orishas.

While some will view animal sacrifice as ugly and wanton, Santeria in no way deploys the practice in this manner. The sacrifice of an animal sustains and nurtures the community in its relationship with the spirit world of the santos and ancestors, maintaining a healthy relationship between them. An ancient practice that has, at one time, been widely followed, animal sacrifice in Santeria serves a vital purpose pivotal to the practice of this descendent of the 4,000-year-old Yoruba Faith. Living at the very heart of the ritual life of Santeria, animal sacrifice has also been enshrined in American law with respect to Santeria.

In 1993, the Church of the Lukumi Babalu Aye v. City of Hialeah established the right of Santeria practitioners to animal sacrifice as a component of its belief system. This opened the door to the 100,000 santeros living in South Florida to practice their religion in peace. The court ruled that the City of Hialeah had impinged on the Constitutional Right to Worship without mitigating factors. In other words, the actions of the City in banning the practices of the Church with respect to animal sacrifice were religiously motivated, with no other underlying purpose. Hialeah had a bone to pick with Santeria just for being there, in other words.

The nature of animal sacrifice in Santeria is so crucial to the practice of the religion (and its symbiotic relationship with the orishas) that removing this aspect of worship would essentially disable the Faith. While many will disagree with much of what I've said here, it's important to remind ourselves that disagreement does not constitute superiority or righteousness. It's mere disagreement. And while animals do, indeed, have rights, so do people, and in the USA, one of those rights is the freedom to worship. In Santeria, animal sacrifice stands as a central pillar, like it or not.

I thank you for joining me for this Introduction to Santeria and hope that I've been able to dispel at least some of the misunderstandings and distortions about this ATR (African Traditional Religion).

Conclusion

Santeria's story is a dramatic one. Its origins in Africa and its arrival in the New World come to us as part of the larger story of the Slave Trade and European Colonialism.

But just as "there are more things in heaven and earth than are dreamed of in your philosophy" (as written in Shakespeare's Hamlet), there are more ways to express devotion to the world of the spirits and the Divine force commanding it than we can understand.

Faith is not just a highly personal thing. Faith is a highly cultural thing. Where the individual fit in culture is often determined by a variety of demographic markers, and religious faith is just one of them. And religious faith grows where it roots. It arises to serve the people found in the context in which it grows, conforming as it pushes up through the rich earth to the needs of those specific people.

In the case of Santeria, there's a back story that needs to be told for the religion to be properly understood and respected for what it is – a religion that came to the shores of the New World under duress. In the minds and hearts of the enslaved, the ancient Yoruba Faith did not die. It lived on, and in the New World, it was transformed.

But it was not, in truth, transformed by the religion of the Colonialists. Rather, it was concealed beneath the symbols and icons of the Roman Catholic Church in order to survive and then flourish in its context. From the cabildos to the streets of Havana and then to the Latin American continent, Santeria grew to become a subject of intense fascination, scorn, distortion, and even envy.

As you've read, Santeria is not black magic or Paganism, or pantheism. It is a religion that grew into a new expression of an ancient religion in Western Africa. Santeria is a story of survival and triumph, and perhaps that's why it has become synonymous (in the minds of some people) with evil. Santeria and other faith systems like it have become living emblems of strength in the face of adversity and the stubborn refusal of the abused to relinquish what's theirs — their beliefs, their culture, and their spirituality.

Santeria, boiled down to its origin story, is a challenge to the colonialist mindset and its insistence that only what it approves of will be permitted on lands that never belonged to the colonizer to start with. Santeria stands as an icon of cultural and spiritual survival and the rejection of imposed standards on those who didn't ask for anything of the sort.

And so, I hope I've been able to convey to you the beauty of Santeria's history. Colonialism couldn't stop it. Communism couldn't stop it. And today, the narrative is changing, and Santeria is taking its place in the world of spirituality as a powerful system of belief that has brought believers comfort in times of oppression, abuse, and enslavement. As it flourishes, I hope I've honored its history.

Thank you for joining me in this exploration of Santeria and some of its core beliefs.

Verum dicatur. Let the truth be told.

References

Afure, E. (2019). *Santeria ritual sacrificial practices in Miami*. Florida International University.

Caribbean religion and anti-colonialism – Caribbean anti-colonial thought archive project. (n.d.). Trincoll.Edu. Retrieved from https://caribbeananti-colonialthoughtarchive.domains.trincoll.edu/caribbean-religion-and-anti-colonialism/

Gage, J. (2010, October 29). *Science of Santeria: Do a little happy trance*. NBC News. https://www.nbcnews.com/id/wbna39915165

Merten, P. (2018, July 31). *In Cuba, Santería flourishes two decades after ban was lifted.* Thegroundtruthproject.Org. https://thegroundtruthproject.org/cuba-santeria-catholicism-religion-flourish-two-decades-freedom-granted/

Ost, B. (2015). *LibGuides: Traditional African religions: Yoruba.* https://research.auctr.edu/c.php?g=404402&p=2752855